HIDDEN TREASURES

20 Interactive Memory Verse Activities

10 Word Search Activities

10 Creative Art Activities with Templates

5 Explosive Science Experiments

Sophie Stokes

Exousia Publishing

Psalm 119:11

Your word I have hidden in my heart that I might not sin against You.

Hidden Treasures © 2014 by Sophie Stokes

Published by Exousia Publishing

Website: www.exousiapublishing.com.au

Email: exousiapublishing@bigpond.com

ISBN: 978-0-9924371-1-4

Scripture taken from the New King James Version. Copyright © 1982 by Thomas Nelson, Inc. Used by permission. All rights reserved.

Acknowledgements

To all my friends who live in far away places, I have especially put this book together for you.

May you be blessed by the contents in this book, but even more, may the One who gives us strength and courage to live our dreams bless you with His loving kindness as you live for Him.

May the children you serve experience His presence in such a way that they will never be the same and forever walk along His paths of righteousness.

Hidden Treasures © 2014 Sophie Stokes

TABLE OF CONTENTS

Introduction

This book is filled with stimulating activities helping students learn God's Word in a fun way. It is a great tool for teachers to use alongside their regular curriculum when teaching kids in school, school scripture, kids church, after-school programs and for those educating their children at home.

Before each memory verse activity is commenced, have the verse printed or photocopy the one provided on an A4 sheet of paper in coloured writing and discuss the verse at a greater length applying it to everyday life. This will enable the student to come to a deeper understanding of God's Word and His love for mankind.

Learning styles of students can fall in one of three categories: Visual, Auditory and Kinesthetic. A student who learns visually benefits from illustrations and presentations, especially when presented in colour. A student who learns by listening and hearing prefers the auditory learning style. The student who needs lots of breaks and likes to move around, remembering what was done more than what was said, is considered to be more of a kinesthetic learner. This book has taken into consideration these three learning styles so that all students are catered for.

Teachers, as your students participate in these activities, you will be able to identify which student's learning style is preferred, helping you to put into place strategies to assist them to learn more effectively according to their style of learning, in other curriculum areas.

20 Memory Verse Activities

Mix It Up!

<u>**Memory Verse**</u> – In the beginning God created the heavens and the earth. Genesis 1:1 (NKJV)

You need

- Blackboard, whiteboard or a large sheet of butcher's paper

- Chalk, white board markers, coloured textas

How many players?

- 2 students

Get Ready

- Write the memory verse twice on the board/paper, changing the spaces between the words so they start or end at different times creating completely new words. For example – Inth ebe ginn in gGo dcre atedt hehe aven san dth eea rt h. Gen es is 1:1.

Action

- Invite 2 students to come to the front while the rest of the students remain in their seats. Explain to them you have written a memory verse on the board/paper and have altered the spaces between the words. Ask them to re-write the verse correctly placing the words in the correct order with the correct spaces in order.

- The student to re-write the memory verse correctly wins!

- Invited students are encouraged to nominate a friend to come up front and help them if they are struggling to work it out.

- When completed, ask all students to read the verse together.

In the beginning God created the heavens and the earth. Genesis 1:1

You've Got Mail

Memory Verse – You shall love the Lord your God with all your heart, with all your soul, and with all your strength. Deuteronomy 6:5 (NKJV)

You need

- 20 pieces of paper that would fit in an envelope or small plastic bag

- Place the completed memory verses in separate envelopes/plastic bags

How many players?

- 4 students

Get Ready

- Write the memory verse twice across the 20 pieces of paper and then place the completed verses in envelopes/plastic bags (one full verse per envelope/bag).

Action

- Invite 4 students to come to the front while the rest of the students remain in their seats. Assign 2 teams.

- Explain to the teams that the object of this game is to pull the pieces of paper out of the envelopes and put together the memory verse in the correct order.

You shall love the Lord your God with all your heart, with all your soul, and with all your strength.

Deuteronomy 6:5

Picture Perfect

Memory Verse – For God so loved the world that He gave His only Son, whoever believes in Him will not die but live forever. John 3:16 (NKJV)

You need

- Blackboard, whiteboard or a large sheet of butcher's paper

- Chalk or markers

How many players?

- 4 students

Get Ready

- On 2 boards or sheets of paper write the memory verse out once, spreading out and leaving space in between words and lines for drawing pictures.

Action

- Invite 4 students to come to the front while the rest of the students remain in their seats.

- Explain to students you have written a memory verse on the board/paper and you would like them to draw a picture under each noun and verb replacing the verb/noun with a picture.

- If the students are struggling to complete the whole verse, encourage them to choose another student seated to replace them and continue the activity.

- Invite the whole class to read the verse together when all words have been drawn.

For God so loved the world that He gave His only Son, whoever believes in Him will not die but live forever. John 3:16

Pizza Wheel

Memory Verse – Be strong and courageous; do not be afraid, or distressed, for the Lord your God is with you wherever you go. Joshua 1:9 (NKJV)

You need

- Cardboard

- Black markers

- Scissors

- Empty pizza box or a large round tray

- Timer

How many players?

- 2 students

Get Ready

- Cut out a large circle of cardboard to fit the pizza box or tray.

- Cut the circle into 10 pieces in pizza style wedges.

- Write 2-3 words on each slice of pizza until you have used all words including name of book.

Action

- Invite 2 students to come to the front while the rest of the students remain in their seats.

- Explain to students the aim of the game is to put all the slices in the correct order to form a pizza and have the verse in the correct order.

- Clarify to them you will be timing them to ascertain who can put the slices back in the box in the correct order the fastest.

- Have the participating student read the verse out loud to the rest of the class.

Be strong and courageous; do not be afraid, or distressed, for the Lord your God is with you wherever you go. Joshua 1:9

Hang out the Washing!

Memory Verse – Delight yourself in the Lord, and He shall give you the desires of your heart. Psalm 37:4 (NKJV)

You need

- Cardboard or paper
- Pegs
- Long piece of rope
- Two chairs
- Markers

How many players?

- 2 students

Get Ready

- Cut out 16 small t-shirt shapes of a small t-shirt from cardboard or paper.
- Write one word of the bible verse on each t-shirt using markers.

- Tie ends of the rope to chairs to make a clothes line, stretching it out firm.

- Place a minimum of 32 pegs in a container next to the line.

Action

- Invite 2 students to come to the front while the rest of the students remain in their seats.

- Explain to participating students that they will be required to peg their t-shirts on the line in the correct order facing the seated students.

- Inform the students you will be timing them, as you will be inviting more students to come to the front and they also will be timed. The students with the fastest time wins.

Delight yourself in the Lord, and He shall give you the desires of your heart.

Psalm 37:4

Flying Objects

<u>**Memory Verse**</u> – Your word I have hidden in my heart, that I might not sin against You. Psalm 119:11 (NKJV)

You need

- 8 paper plates

- Coloured markers

How many players?

- All students

Get Ready

- Write two words of the bible verse in order on each paper plate.

Action

- Explain to the class that you will be throwing the paper plate out to them like a Frisbee and if they hear their name, they need to stand up and catch it, as it will be heading towards them.

- Invite the catchers to come to the front and line up in the correct order of the verse.

- Once the verse is in the correct order, invite the students who have remained in their seats to say the verse together out loud.

Your word I have

hidden in my heart,

that I might not sin

against You.

Psalm 119:11

Hidden Treasures

Memory Verse – In all your ways acknowledge Him, and He shall direct your paths. Proverbs 3:6 (NKJV)

You need

- 14 squares of paper 15cm x 10cm

- Coloured markers

- Old newspaper scrunched up

- 2 small wastebaskets or buckets

How many players?

- 6 students

Get Ready

- Write two words of the bible verse on each square of paper. Do this twice, so you have two full verses.

- Fill wastebaskets with scrunched up newspaper and fold the bible verse papers and put in baskets – place one full verse in one basket, and the second verse in the other basket.

- Assign a basket to each team.

Action

- Invite 6 students to come to the front while the rest of the students remain in their seats. Assign 2 teams of 3.

- Explain to the students that they will be required to look through the wastebaskets and find the bible verses written on plain paper. Once found, they will pull them out, open them up and line them up in the correct order.

In all your ways acknowledge Him, and He shall direct your paths.

Proverbs 3:6

T-Shirt Line Up

Memory Verse – The grass withers, the flower fades, but the word of our God stands forever. Isaiah 40:8 (NKJV)

You need

- 10 large t-shirts or collect some old, plain shirts

- Coloured markers

How many players?

- 10 students

Get Ready

- Write the verse on the t-shirts in phrases with the markers, a couple of words per t-shirt.

- Place the shirts in a box.

Action

- Invite 10 students to come to the front while the rest of the students remain in their seats.

- Explain to participating students they are required to choose a shirt out of the box and put it on.

- Once everyone has their shirt on, they are to form two groups displaying the verse in the correct order.

- Invite the seated students to offer suggestions to the participants of where they may be best placed.

- Inform the participating students they will be timed as to how fast they can form the verse in the correct order.

- Invite a seated student to stand up where they are seated and read out the verse to the rest of the class.

- Direct students back to their seats. Invite 10 new students to come forward and have them repeat the activity. Challenge them to get the verse in order faster than the last group.

The grass withers, the flower fades, but the word of our God stands forever.

Isaiah 40:8

Burger Run

Memory Verse – For I know the thoughts I think toward you, thoughts of peace and not of evil, to give you a future and a hope. Jeremiah 29:11 (NKJV)

You need

- Coloured construction paper

- Scissors

- Coloured markers

How many players?

- 4 students

Get Ready

- Cut out coloured cardboard out in the shape of a burger bun, a meat pattie, a slice of cheese, a lettuce leaf and a slice of tomato. Cut two of everything.

- Write on each one 3 or 4 words of the verse until you use up all the words and all the cutouts.

- Make sure you write the beginning and ends of the verse on the burger buns. Mix them up in two separate piles.

Action

- Invite 4 students to come to the front while the rest of the students remain in their seats. Assign 2 teams of 2.

- Explain to participating students these hamburgers need to be assembled in the correct order.

- On the word, *go* the teams will begin to assemble the burgers according to the order of the bible verse.

- When both teams have finished, have team 1 read out what team 2 have put together and then ask team 2 to read what team 1 has put together.

For I know the thoughts I think toward you, thoughts of peace and not of evil, to give you a future and a hope.

Jeremiah 29:11

Guess the Word

Memory Verse – If anyone is in Christ, he is a new creation; old things have passed away; behold, all things have become new. 2 Corinthians 5:17 (NKJV)

You need

- 10 sheets of A4 plain white paper

- Coloured markers

How many players?

- 10 students

Get Ready

- Write the verse on the paper using one sheet of paper every 2–3 words.

Action

- Invite 10 students to come to the front while the rest of the students remain in their seats. Hand each of them a sheet of paper.

- Direct them to line up facing the rest of the class.

- Ask the students who have remained in their seats to put their hand up if anyone needs to be re-shuffled. Ask one of the seated students to come forward and re-arrange according to the correct order.

- When in the correct order, have the whole class recite the verse and volunteer can sit back down.

- Turn one player around so that their word cannot be seen.

- Have all students recite the verse with the missing word.

- Continue turning the students around and reciting the verse until there are no words showing.

- Ask for a student who is seated to recite the verse.

- Have all the participating students turn around and face the seated students and together ask everyone to recite the verse.

If anyone is in Christ, he is a new creation; old things have passed away; behold, all things have become new.

2 Corinthians 5:17

Food for Thought

Memory Verse – I am the bread of life. He who comes to me shall never hunger, and he who believes in Me shall never thirst. John 6:35 (NKJV)

You need

- 2 empty boxes of biscuits or cereal

- 10 sheets of A4 paper, cut in half

- Coloured markers

How many players?

- 2 students

Get Ready

- Write the bible verse, three words at a time on the paper cut in half - making two lots of verses.

- Place each set into the separate boxes.

Action

- Invite 2 students to come to the front and stand next to a box while the rest of the students remain in their seats.

- Explain to participating students the verse is in the box and they need to pull it out and place the verse in the correct order.

- When both students have placed their verse in order, ask them together to read out the verse.

- If there are any discrepancies, invite a seated student to correct the discrepancy.

I am the bread of life.
He who comes to me
shall never hunger,
and he who believes
in Me shall never
thirst. John 6:35

Stack a Can

Memory Verse – If you love me, keep My commandments. John 14:15 (NKJV)

You need

- 5 empty cans of soft drink

- 5 small slips of paper

- Adhesive tape

- Coloured markers

How many players?

- 2 students

Get Ready

- Write the bible verse, two words at a time on the paper with the reference on a separate one.

- Attach verse phrases to each can.

Action

- Invite 2 students to come to the front while the rest of the students remain in their seats.

- Explain to the students together they are to stack the cans on top of each other in the correct order with the verse starting from the bottom. Ask them to face the rest of the class while they do this.

- Time them and see how fast they can stack the verse in the correct order.

- When all cans are stacked, invite a seated student to read out the verse and determine if it has been placed in the correct order.

- When correctly read, reshuffle all cans and invite 2 new students to come forward and participate in the activity.

If you love me, keep

My commandments.

John 14:15

Newspaper Collage

Memory Verse – I am the vine, you are the branches. He who abides in Me, and I in him, bears much fruit; for without Me you can do nothing. John 15:5 (NKJV)

You need

- Newspapers or magazines

- Scissors

- Glue sticks

- Large sheets of plain paper

- Butcher's paper, blackboard or whiteboard

- Coloured markers or chalk

How many players?

- Assign all students into groups of 4 or 5

Get Ready

- Give each group one newspaper/magazine, 2 or 3 pairs of scissors, one glue stick and one large sheet of plain paper.

- On a blackboard, whiteboard or large sheet of butcher's paper, display the verse.

Action

- Invite students to gather in groups of 4 or 5, moving their chairs together and placing one desk in the middle of them.

- Explain to students they are going to make a collage of the verse and will be cutting out letters or pictures they find in the newspaper or magazine and will glue them in the correct order on the paper to represent the verse.

- Encourage students to be creative and to 'think outside the square' when looking for representations.

I am the vine, you are the branches. He who abides in Me, and I in him, bears much fruit; for without Me you can do nothing.

John 15:5

Jigsaw Puzzle

<u>Memory Verse</u> – For I am not ashamed of the gospel of Christ, for it is the power of God to salvation for everyone who believes. Romans 1:16 (NKJV)

You need

- Two large sheets of construction cardboard, in different colours

- Coloured markers

How many players?

- 4 students

Get Ready

- Write the memory verse on both sheets of cardboard.

- Cut out cardboard like a puzzle, cutting words in half and all different shapes and sizes.

- Place each puzzle on two separate tables ready to construct.

Action

- Invite students to come to the front while the rest of the students remain in their seats.

- Explain to participating students the memory verse is a puzzle and like all puzzles they need to find the correct pieces that fit together.

- Have the players stand behind their table, which has the puzzle pieces sitting on top. Together with their teammate, they will assemble the puzzle. If they are struggling, choose a seated student to come forward to assist them.

- The team that puts their puzzle together in the correct order first, wins.

- Ask the winning team to read out their verse to the class.

For I am not ashamed of the gospel of Christ, for it is the power of God to salvation for everyone who believes.

Romans 1:16

Backwards

Memory Verse – God demonstrated His own love toward us, in that while we were still sinners, Christ died for us. Romans 5:8 (NKJV)

You need

- Blackboard, whiteboard or a large sheet of butcher's paper

- Coloured markers

How many players?

- 2 students

Get Ready

- Write out the bible verse on board or butcher's paper, backwards.

Action

- Invite 2 students to come to the front while the rest of the students remain in their seats.

- Explain to participating students you were having a bad day this morning and you became a little disoriented and wrote the memory verse backwards and now you need their help to correct this.

- Invite them to re-write the verse for you, in the correct order.

God demonstrated His own love toward us, in that while we were still sinners, Christ died for us.

Romans 5:8

Straw Relay

<u>Memory Verse</u> – I can do all things through Christ who strengthens me. Philippians 4:13 (NKJV)

You need

- 1 box of tissues

- Coloured markers

- 1 packet of drinking straws

How many players?

- 6 students

Get Ready

- On each tissue write out 2 words of the bible verse, creating two verses.

- Place the tissues on the floor at one end of the room in two different groups and the straws at the other end of the room in two different groups.

Action

- Invite 6 students to come to the front while the rest of the students remain in their seats.

- Explain to them each player will run to the other end of the room with a straw in their hand. When they get there they will place the straw in their mouth. Leaning over one tissue, they will breathe in the straw and suck up the tissue to attach it to the end of the straw.

- With straw in mouth, and tissue attached, they will run back to their starting point and tag the next player.

- The next player will run down to tissues and do the same until all the players have had a turn and all the tissues have been brought to the starting end.

- The team will then line up the verse in the correct order.

I can do all things through Christ who strengthens me.

Philippians 4:13

Use Your Nose

Memory Verse – Pursue love, and desire spiritual gifts, but especially that you may prophesy. 1 Corinthians 14:1 (NKJV)

You need

- 26 small pieces of paper

- Coloured markers

- Two jars of face cream such as Sorbelene

How many players?

- 8 students

Get Ready

- Write the verse across the pieces of paper, creating two verses.

- Place 2 chairs at one end of the room and place one group of verses on each chair and 2 chairs at the other end of the room with a bottle of cream on each.

Action

- Invite 8 students to come to the front while the rest of the students remain in their seats. Assign 2 teams of 4.

- Explain to students that they will be using their nose to collect the verses with the cream they are going to put on their nose.

- Invite them to line up in their teams next to one of the chairs and to apply the cream to their nose.

- Tell them they will run to the other end of the room with the cream on their nose, put their nose to the paper on the chair and only collect one piece on their nose. They will run back and tag their team member.

- The new player runs to the other end and repeats what the first team member just did until they have collected all their verse.

- They will remove verse from their nose and place all the words in the correct order.

Pursue love, and desire spiritual gifts, but especially that you may prophesy.

1 Corinthians 14:1

Know Your Vowels

Memory Verse – My grace is sufficient for you, for My strength is made perfect in weakness. 2 Corinthians 12:9 (NKJV)

You need

- Blackboard, whiteboard or butcher's paper
- Coloured markers, chalk

How many players?

- All students

Get Ready

- Write out the verse on the board or butcher's paper.
- Leave all the vowels out of the words, leaving a space for them.

Action

- Explain to the students that you have written out the verse but have left out the vowels.

- Ask for volunteers to put their hands up and suggest which vowel should go where until the verse is completed correctly.

- Repeat this activity by writing out the verse again and this time leaving out some consonants. You may even like to replace a consonant with a picture. For example if you left out the 'c' you can draw a picture of the sea or eyes to depict being able to see.

My grace is sufficient for you, for My strength is made perfect in weakness.

2 Corinthians 12:9

Gone Fishing

Memory Verse – Follow me and I will make you fishers of men. Matthew 4:19 (NKJV)

You need

- A small fishing rod or stick to represent a fishing rod

- String or fishing line

- Cardboard

- 12 small magnets and adhesive tape

- Markers

- A low tub

How many players?

- 2 students

Get Ready

- Cut out 10 small fish and write one word of the verse on each fish.

- Attach the string to the rod and place a magnet on end like you would for a lead weight when fishing.

- Place one magnet at the mouth of each fish using adhesive tape.

- Place all the fish in the tub.

Action

- Invite 2 students to come to the front while the rest of the students remain in their seats.

- Explain to participating students the aim of the game is to 'catch' the fish and place them in the correct order of the verse.

- One student will 'catch' and the other one will put the verse in order.

- When all fish have been caught and placed in order, invite the catcher to read out the verse to the rest of the class.

- A timer can be used to time the team and see who can complete this task the fastest.

Follow me and I will make you fishers of men.

Matthew 4:19

Balloon Pop

Memory Verse - Do you not know that you are the temple of God and the Spirit of God dwells in you? 1 Corinthians 3:16 (NKJV)

You need

- 10 balloons (have a few spare in case of burst balloons before the game commences)
- 10 small pieces of paper
- 10 pieces of string about 50cm long
- 1 red marker and 1 black/blue marker

How many players?

- 10 students

Get Ready

- Write the verse on five pieces of paper, twice, one group with red and the other group with black/blue markers.

- Slip the folded paper into the balloons and inflate. Tie off.

- Attach the string to each of the balloons.

Action

- Invite 10 students to come to the front while the rest of the students remain in their seats. Assign the two teams a colour, either red or black/blue.

- Instruct the students to tie the string attached to the balloon around their ankle.

- The object of the game is to burst each other's balloon and find their tags (which will be red or black/blue).

- They are to collect their pieces of paper with the bible verse words in their team colours and stand in the correct order of the verse.

- Invite one of the players on each team to read out their verse.

Do you not know that

you are the temple of

God and the Spirit of

God dwells in you?

1 Corinthians 3:16

10 *Word Search*

Activities

Where It All Started!

In the beginning God created the heavens and the earth. Genesis 1:1 (NKJV).

He made the world in six days and rested on the seventh. It was without form having no animals, no birds, no people and no sun and moon on it. But then God spoke and brought everything into being.

Find these words – look up, look down, look across and look diagonally, backwards and forwards.

Adam	Declared	God	Night	Spoke	Wet
Beginning	Earth	Good	Planets	Stars	
Birds	Empty	Heavens	Plants	Sun	
Created	Eve	Light	Rested	Tree of Life	
Dark	Fruit	Moon	Serpent	Universe	
Day	Garden	New	Seventh	Void	

Write below any additional words you find and compare with your friend.

E	A	R	T	H	A	A	D	M	S	I	N	D	E	S	A	T	H	A	V
T	I	U	R	F	D	E	C	L	A	R	E	D	F	T	R	O	M	O	N
I	A	D	A	M	O	P	T	M	W	I	W	I	R	A	L	V	I	L	A
N	J	G	T	O	N	O	H	M	Y	W	O	R	E	R	W	D	A	I	Z
L	I	G	H	T	A	W	G	B	N	G	O	D	E	S	O	V	C	V	B
N	O	O	M	J	N	F	I	H	J	O	E	M	P	T	Y	N	O	I	E
G	B	T	K	A	T	I	N	G	O	P	E	R	D	D	E	C	L	K	Y
A	C	E	L	B	D	R	B	E	G	N	E	W	O	K	H	E	O	V	D
R	F	L	M	E	T	E	E	V	O	I	P	D	R	A	R	P	K	O	S
D	D	E	N	G	L	R	T	E	I	G	H	A	M	T	S	P	O	K	C
E	E	V	Q	I	S	U	E	S	O	M	D	O	C	O	N	B	I	R	G
N	T	I	W	N	D	S	P	E	E	F	L	A	S	D	R	I	B	N	O
G	A	S	C	N	T	S	N	I	S	R	L	G	A	H	T	S	F	R	O
H	E	I	X	I	U	T	Y	E	S	S	H	I	P	S	R	A	S	M	D
T	R	S	T	N	A	L	P	O	W	E	T	A	F	D	A	U	N	S	T
N	C	O	Y	G	O	I	N	T	G	B	A	E	T	E	S	P	E	U	E
E	H	N	J	W	Y	E	A	R	T	U	N	I	N	V	R	E	V	E	X
V	I	T	M	A	N	L	E	Y	E	S	T	E	R	A	T	C	A	N	N
E	U	H	D	N	A	D	T	N	E	P	R	E	S	O	L	A	E	E	U
S	A	E	B	E	S	R	E	V	I	N	U	W	E	T	O	P	H	V	S

A Heart After God

You shall love the Lord your God with all your heart, with all your soul, and with all your strength. Deuteronomy 6:5 (NKJV).

David loved God with all his heart; despite His failings God spoke highly of David and announced that he had a heart after God, which means he pursued God with all his heart, soul and strength.

Find these words – look up, look down, look across and look diagonally, backwards and forwards.

Courage	God	Love	Spoke	Victory
David	Goliath	Loving	Strength	
Deuteronomy	Heart	Mighty	Success	
Fail	Joy	Psalms	Soul	
Faith	Kindness	Pursued	Truth	

Write below any additional words you find and compare with your friend.

A	Q	T	R	U	T	H	P	E	A	C	E	J	O	Y	P	B	R	L	T
P	U	R	S	U	E	D	T	S	F	B	A	B	Y	L	A	O	D	O	S
B	A	J	O	F	H	G	S	E	O	A	T	A	P	I	T	R	E	V	M
M	S	A	G	R	I	O	V	L	O	H	I	S	P	V	I	N	U	I	L
I	T	C	D	O	K	O	X	F	T	E	E	T	O	I	E	I	T	N	A
G	R	K	L	W	L	D	U	C	B	N	V	I	H	N	N	N	E	G	S
H	O	T	S	I	J	I	Y	O	A	E	O	C	S	G	C	A	R	K	F
T	N	R	P	N	K	N	A	N	L	O	B	A	G	I	E	S	O	I	H
Y	A	E	A	D	L	E	Z	T	D	A	V	I	D	N	X	T	N	N	O
C	U	C	C	O	T	R	A	E	H	V	A	S	E	T	Z	A	O	D	R
D	T	C	E	W	M	S	B	R	L	I	E	W	L	I	A	F	M	N	S
E	Q	O	S	U	N	S	D	O	V	T	S	T	K	H	U	B	Y	E	E
S	G	S	E	K	O	P	S	L	T	A	I	I	K	E	C	L	C	S	S
U	J	N	H	P	A	F	M	I	U	L	R	M	Y	L	O	E	H	S	A
C	X	C	I	Q	N	R	U	G	B	Y	G	E	R	I	U	O	A	N	B
C	Z	V	P	W	Y	U	D	C	V	I	O	T	O	G	R	D	R	N	C
E	Q	B	N	E	I	I	N	X	Z	C	D	O	T	H	A	H	I	E	L
S	R	E	H	T	G	N	E	R	T	S	E	L	C	T	G	N	O	E	U
S	E	T	I	R	K	T	H	G	I	R	F	P	I	O	E	I	T	U	O
F	D	I	M	L	O	V	E	E	U	Q	G	O	V	N	X	K	S	Q	S

Love Rules

For God so loved the world that He gave His only Son, whoever believes in Him will not die but
live forever. John 3:16 (NKJV).

It was in the middle of the day but suddenly it became very dark and a storm was brewing. Jesus then said, "It is finished!" The earth shook and the veil in the temple tore in two.

Find these words – look up, look down, look across and look diagonally, backwards and forwards.

Afternoon	Crucified	Gave	Mercy	Storm
Believe	Darkness	Grace	Mother	Surrender
Brewing	Dice	It is finished	Saviour	Two
Confess	Disciples	Jesus	Shook	Veil
Cross	Earthquake	Love	Son	Vinegar

Write below any additional words you find and compare with your friend.

G	Z	D	Q	V	E	I	L	E	D	C	V	D	L	O	V	E	F	G	S
A	A	H	I	L	L	T	O	R	I	R	P	A	V	E	S	N	Y	V	U
S	F	V	T	S	N	H	E	E	S	O	V	A	N	H	O	O	I	O	R
T	E	O	E	W	C	T	R	W	C	S	I	L	O	G	B	N	A	L	R
R	S	O	N	A	W	O	G	I	I	S	V	O	I	I	E	K	F	C	E
O	R	N	O	O	R	E	V	N	P	L	K	I	V	G	E	S	T	O	N
J	E	S	U	S	E	M	E	G	L	Y	E	N	A	N	S	B	E	N	D
N	N	P	S	L	H	I	H	A	E	S	R	R	I	T	D	E	R	F	E
D	A	R	K	N	E	S	S	T	S	P	E	Y	L	E	E	A	N	E	R
O	B	O	W	E	T	S	T	S	O	I	E	T	H	H	H	S	O	S	W
S	A	R	E	S	U	P	N	O	H	D	S	S	E	I	T	U	O	S	Y
M	T	T	N	A	O	H	A	U	E	R	I	E	N	M	Y	C	N	I	R
I	Y	O	N	U	S	E	E	I	H	N	O	H	O	O	A	C	O	N	E
C	S	M	R	S	A	R	F	Y	I	I	T	E	Y	T	M	R	T	M	E
L	T	A	I	M	I	I	C	F	T	T	A	R	H	Y	U	L	E	V
I	O	C	E	T	C	N	S	T	F	E	N	R	E	E	R	O	U	R	E
G	C	Q	I	U	L	I	O	H	O	C	A	T	V	R	E	I	F	C	I
H	K	U	R	R	T	D	N	L	D	A	W	S	E	C	T	V	S	Y	L
A	T	C	A	I	A	I	A	A	N	R	E	O	I	C	N	A	S	E	E
E	A	R	T	H	Q	U	A	K	E	G	W	D	D	O	U	S	E	V	B

A New Day

Be strong and courageous; do not be afraid, or distressed, for the Lord your God is with you wherever you go. Joshua 1:9 (NKJV).

After Moses died, Joshua was given the authority to lead the people of Israel into the Promised Land. It was not going to be easy, but one thing Joshua knew and that was that God promised to be with him.

Find these words – look up, look down, look across and look diagonally, backwards and forwards.

Afraid	Fire	Joshua	Pharaoh	Strong
Angel	Giants	Jericho	Promised	Walls
Authority	Given	Land	Rahab	Whenever
Canaan	Holy	Moses	Sheep	Wilderness
Courageous	Israel	Passover	Spies	Zion

Write below any additional words you find and compare with your friend.

H	O	L	Y	A	Y	G	S	F	A	R	Z	R	E	V	E	R	E	H	W
I	C	O	B	I	H	A	P	S	Y	U	V	F	X	F	G	X	Q	X	C
S	O	M	E	N	E	B	I	H	A	J	T	Q	A	C	N	T	H	R	E
A	S	T	R	O	N	G	E	E	U	H	Z	H	B	D	R	H	T	A	P
U	T	E	I	U	W	C	S	I	P	D	G	W	O	E	B	H	O	H	R
H	R	H	J	A	H	D	X	R	H	R	X	C	M	R	E	E	T	A	O
S	E	E	S	K	Q	E	O	D	S	E	F	B	O	L	I	M	N	B	M
O	V	C	I	F	L	M	R	E	D	H	K	V	I	I	L	T	I	D	I
J	O	M	N	B	I	F	P	D	G	I	V	E	N	V	P	O	Y	S	D
O	S	E	N	S	H	R	O	X	S	S	E	N	R	E	D	L	I	W	E
U	S	M	E	I	M	G	E	H	O	V	H	G	I	A	N	T	S	D	S
R	A	D	L	N	I	T	F	G	J	H	O	A	R	A	H	P	D	L	U
G	P	A	O	T	J	P	A	D	I	A	R	F	A	E	O	U	N	A	O
O	N	E	I	O	H	C	I	R	E	J	H	P	E	E	H	S	A	N	E
D	I	V	A	L	Q	X	N	D	K	J	A	B	T	R	E	T	T	E	G
W	D	I	E	E	Z	B	A	P	L	K	S	O	A	Y	P	W	A	A	A
H	N	G	V	A	M	D	A	I	N	L	E	R	E	O	A	R	P	W	R
O	N	L	L	R	I	H	N	B	O	D	S	N	T	L	A	O	Y	X	U
A	A	E	A	S	N	E	A	V	I	B	O	E	L	H	R	F	G	B	O
I	S	H	S	I	B	Y	C	Q	Z	X	M	S	P	C	U	E	Y	Q	C

A Delightful Queen

Delight yourself in the Lord, and He shall give you the desires of your heart. Psalm 37:4 (NKJV).

Queen Esther delighted herself in the matters of God. Her people were at risk of being wiped out, but instead of fretting and causing a fuss, she waited on God to give her the go ahead to approach the King and receive his favour and protect her people were protected.

Find these words – look up, look down, look across and look diagonally, backwards and forwards.

Army	Desires	Hanging	Jews	Pleased
Beauty	Esther	Heart	Mordecai	Queen
Chosen	Favour	Honour	Palace	Royal
Delight	Feast	Jewels	Persecution	Rule

Write below any additional words you find and compare with your friend.

Q	O	W	R	A	O	D	J	E	W	S	P	G	W	A	M	S	P	X	M
A	U	A	U	R	Y	A	Z	B	K	H	G	T	U	P	N	L	E	O	B
H	T	E	L	T	S	A	N	C	T	U	A	R	Y	A	F	M	R	Y	K
T	S	A	E	F	T	L	V	S	A	V	E	S	V	Z	W	D	S	T	G
B	S	R	P	N	H	L	P	L	E	A	S	E	D	N	E	L	E	R	A
E	D	E	A	F	E	W	O	B	W	O	X	W	M	C	T	G	C	O	R
A	I	D	R	O	A	S	G	A	F	L	H	R	A	O	W	V	U	S	M
U	V	S	T	I	T	K	T	S	D	K	N	I	G	H	A	L	T	W	Y
T	I	G	Y	H	S	N	C	H	I	Y	I	T	F	O	S	D	I	B	S
Y	D	O	E	I	A	E	B	P	E	W	C	N	X	D	P	J	O	W	P
D	G	I	L	E	N	D	V	S	R	P	V	G	S	H	Y	N	R	F	
E	N	D	S	S	L	O	X	K	G	M	E	O	B	Z	I	P	S	L	O
A	U	A	T	E	C	A	L	A	P	Y	L	T	J	E	W	E	L	S	K
T	I	M	I	N	G	W	A	S	O	A	N	W	R	V	F	T	W	B	G
R	S	R	R	G	L	T	F	E	F	W	V	H	O	N	O	U	R	M	E
T	T	U	B	L	W	N	O	C	H	O	S	E	N	G	Z	C	P	V	N
R	Y	O	B	A	I	A	D	A	R	G	U	C	O	Y	W	K	A	G	O
A	A	V	A	Y	L	E	I	L	O	T	P	D	E	L	I	G	H	T	R
E	H	A	E	O	L	E	E	A	S	L	X	I	M	S	H	E	W	F	H
H	T	F	H	R	S	S	H	P	H	A	N	G	I	N	G	Z	P	C	T

Set Apart

Your word I have hidden in my heart, that I might not sin against You.
Psalm 119:11 (NKJV).

Before Samson was born, an angel visited his mother to tell her she would have a son. This son had special calling on his life; he saves Israel from the Philistines. He was to be a Nazirite, promising to serve God alone.

Find these words – look up, look down, look across and look diagonally, backwards and forwards.

Angel	Destroy	Mother	Serve	Visited
Apart	Haircut	Nazirite	Set	Vow
Calling	Heart	Philistines	Son	Word
Dedicate	Hidden	Power	Strong	
Delilah	Lion	Samson	Temple	

Write below any additional words you find and compare with your friend.

N	C	B	E	V	R	E	S	N	H	I	A	X	S	O	N	A	L	Z	W
A	A	G	Y	U	P	A	E	S	T	C	N	T	P	V	B	E	I	V	A
B	C	Z	H	Y	U	G	H	T	H	E	G	Q	N	U	E	D	O	G	P
M	B	F	I	O	O	A	W	R	W	B	E	W	D	A	L	L	N	J	Q
C	O	E	T	R	R	T	D	O	A	N	L	J	E	W	A	B	C	W	G
B	S	T	C	U	I	H	N	N	V	I	S	I	T	E	D	R	T	E	N
L	L	L	H	S	H	T	A	G	T	W	U	B	D	S	H	I	V	M	I
I	I	A	O	E	T	E	E	Y	E	O	S	G	E	Y	O	T	J	B	L
N	W	R	M	A	R	F	E	O	R	R	E	N	I	E	T	T	D	H	L
D	E	N	E	Y	E	L	P	M	E	T	I	V	R	E	W	O	P	A	A
F	N	H	I	V	O	W	R	U	S	T	A	P	C	S	Y	A	H	I	C
G	O	I	W	S	L	I	E	G	S	D	M	D	R	O	W	I	E	R	W
E	O	D	M	T	R	R	H	I	Y	T	W	Q	A	J	N	N	T	C	J
T	N	D	A	H	O	E	L	T	O	R	I	G	T	U	R	B	R	U	Z
A	M	E	I	O	G	H	T	H	U	A	H	O	E	N	U	Y	U	T	V
C	L	N	R	D	P	I	E	R	W	P	A	O	D	A	O	P	T	G	Q
I	K	O	O	A	U	W	B	O	I	A	L	D	T	C	Y	S	H	A	P
D	J	D	E	S	T	R	O	Y	T	O	L	W	O	E	T	E	M	R	D
E	H	T	F	Y	O	I	L	H	E	A	R	T	G	T	H	W	J	A	W
D	E	L	I	L	A	H	L	G	S	N	Y	Z	P	V	B	O	N	X	S

His Ways are Higher

In all your ways acknowledge Him, and He shall direct your paths. Proverbs 3:6 (NKJV).

Ruth was a faithful woman trusting God to see her through the difficulties she encountered in her life. God took care of her and blessed her.

Find these words – look up, look down, look across and look diagonally, backwards and forwards.

Acknowledge	Faithful	Home	Paths	Trust
Blessed	Field	Hope	Proverbs	Ways
Boaz	Future	Love	Roof	Wheat
Care	God	Marriage	Ruth	Woman
Direct	Grain	Naomi	Travel	

Write below any additional words you find and compare with your friend.

M	A	R	R	I	A	H	P	A	T	H	S	H	B	H	T	S	U	R	T
Q	G	O	U	R	B	O	T	O	D	R	A	O	O	G	W	I	W	I	N
W	R	O	E	N	R	M	H	G	L	I	A	M	T	O	E	L	I	L	I
E	O	F	A	I	I	E	N	Y	Z	P	C	U	E	P	O	H	T	A	R
D	F	O	S	O	D	T	C	F	A	J	R	I	T	D	H	L	R	C	R
D	M	G	T	M	E	A	F	O	U	M	V	E	I	R	D	A	D	O	G
I	T	R	S	N	R	E	E	E	N	H	O	N	M	E	V	F	L	M	X
N	S	A	A	E	S	M	L	O	V	E	I	W	B	E	F	E	N	E	V
G	A	C	N	M	M	O	A	M	I	A	D	T	L	S	N	E	A	F	R
C	F	E	D	Y	A	C	S	I	O	V	E	F	U	I	A	F	E	U	Q
E	G	D	E	L	W	O	N	K	C	A	R	O	S	S	L	R	T	T	W
L	K	I	T	X	I	N	T	T	N	O	H	R	G	O	D	H	M	U	P
W	H	E	A	T	D	E	S	A	O	H	T	M	D	Y	B	O	O	R	Z
E	A	S	H	I	S	B	T	R	R	E	C	E	V	T	L	M	T	E	U
B	E	S	E	Z	R	M	O	E	D	J	E	A	O	T	E	Y	E	C	O
R	R	U	P	E	G	S	R	B	A	Y	R	D	L	H	S	O	S	L	Y
A	B	F	V	S	R	M	E	M	I	B	I	L	Y	E	S	U	O	O	S
T	N	O	A	Y	O	O	M	E	N	D	D	E	M	D	E	C	L	S	Y
I	R	F	M	A	R	R	I	A	G	E	T	I	D	E	D	O	C	E	A
P	O	I	R	T	L	U	F	H	T	I	A	F	N	V	I	M	E	T	W

Solid as a Rock

The grass withers, the flower fades, but the word of our God stands forever. Isaiah 40:8 (NKJV).

When Jesus went out to the wilderness to be alone with His Father, the enemy came to him and wanted to seduce Him to do what he wanted. But each time He responded with the word of God. Jesus knew the word thoroughly and was ready to give an answer from God's Word.

Find these words – look up, look down, look across and look diagonally, backwards and forwards.

Alone	Bread	Flower	Mountain	Truth
Answer	Enemy	Forever	Seduce	Wilderness
Authority	Fades	Grass	Stands	Wither
Bible	Father	Jesus	Temptation	Word

Write below any additional words you find and compare with your friend.

M	F	A	D	E	S	E	D	E	C	R	F	V	S	T	G	B	F	Y	A
O	Q	A	Z	W	S	X	I	Y	H	N	U	V	J	M	I	L	K	O	U
U	L	P	Q	A	Z	B	W	S	X	E	E	D	C	R	O	F	V	T	T
N	G	B	Y	H	L	N	U	J	M	R	G	I	K	W	O	L	P	Q	H
T	A	Z	W	E	D	C	R	F	O	V	R	F	E	V	T	G	B	Y	O
A	Y	H	N	U	W	T	J	F	M	I	A	R	K	O	L	R	F	P	R
I	Q	A	Z	E	I	W	E	S	X	E	S	D	C	R	E	F	O	V	I
N	T	G	N	B	L	Y	H	M	N	U	S	J	M	W	I	K	R	O	T
L	P	O	Q	A	D	S	Z	W	P	S	X	E	S	D	C	R	E	F	Y
V	L	T	G	B	E	E	Y	H	N	T	U	N	J	M	I	K	V	O	L
A	P	Q	A	Z	R	D	W	S	X	E	A	D	C	R	Y	M	E	N	E
R	O	U	G	H	N	U	M	E	A	N	T	T	G	H	E	Y	R	C	E
M	I	N	T	A	E	C	S	T	A	N	D	S	I	T	I	N	T	H	E
C	A	P	A	T	S	E	T	O	D	A	Y	S	O	O	N	M	O	O	N
J	E	S	U	S	S	G	R	N	R	R	L	O	N	G	N	T	I	M	E
T	H	E	H	O	F	F	E	S	O	E	B	O	T	T	O	M	A	R	T
N	T	H	T	R	O	W	H	A	T	H	W	O	R	D	F	I	S	H	J
L	I	P	U	S	I	P	T	O	F	T	T	O	D	A	Y	J	F	R	S
M	T	B	R	D	A	X	I	G	O	A	T	L	O	N	G	S	O	N	G
S	I	T	T	M	I	T	W	O	F	F	B	O	M	B	D	A	E	R	B

Success In Him

For I know the thoughts I think toward you, thoughts of peace and not of evil, to give you a future and a hope. Jeremiah 29:11 (NKJV).

Samuel was a gift from God. His mother, Hannah could not fall pregnant for a long time but she sought the help of God and He answered her prayers. He gave her success in her future because she put her hope and trust in Him.

Find these words – look up, look down, look across and look diagonally, backwards and forwards.

Answered	Future	Hope	Obeyed	Pregnant	Temple
Baby	Gift	Jeremiah	Peace	Priest	
Thoughts					
Bold	Hannah	Listened	Petition	Success	Victory
Eli	Help	Ministry	Prayers	Samuel	Voice

Write below any additional words you find and compare with your friend.

L	P	L	O	K	E	M	A	I	Y	J	E	L	P	M	E	T	N	U	P
I	S	E	X	P	D	M	N	R	B	C	F	S	T	V	G	Y	B	H	R
S	Z	A	O	Q	W	I	S	E	A	D	C	A	R	F	V	T	G	B	E
T	G	H	R	O	W	N	W	M	B	G	O	M	M	O	A	T	J	H	G
E	T	H	R	O	W	I	E	D	A	W	N	U	H	E	L	P	G	A	N
N	Q	D	A	M	V	S	R	K	E	E	P	E	C	A	M	E	H	I	A
E	F	O	R	G	E	T	E	E	T	H	E	L	E	C	A	E	P	M	N
D	T	O	I	H	E	R	D	V	C	T	P	K	B	D	A	W	N	E	T
T	O	F	G	O	T	Y	P	M	E	I	H	A	N	N	A	H	I	R	I
I	T	L	E	T	E	A	R	R	A	W	O	B	O	T	T	O	M	E	D
D	A	W	N	W	R	T	A	B	E	E	N	V	S	E	V	E	N	J	B
M	E	A	N	T	U	T	Y	D	O	W	N	O	F	T	S	E	I	R	P
K	E	E	P	I	T	D	E	R	S	P	Y	S	G	R	E	A	T	N	E
H	E	L	P	G	U	T	R	P	I	E	S	I	T	I	P	C	U	P	T
Z	D	L	O	P	F	R	S	L	I	T	I	G	T	H	E	R	E	T	I
E	Y	E	I	O	J	O	B	E	Z	I	T	I	M	E	G	O	A	T	T
Y	O	U	N	T	O	D	V	H	Z	T	L	I	M	P	R	U	G	H	I
E	F	O	G	B	O	L	D	E	T	Y	O	W	M	S	U	Q	O	E	O
B	F	B	O	H	G	K	M	L	V	V	I	C	T	O	R	Y	U	H	N
O	B	I	T	I	P	S	S	E	C	C	U	S	U	R	K	A	R	K	T

Brand New

If anyone is in Christ, he is a new creation; old things have passed away; behold, all things have become new. 2 Corinthians 5:17 (NKJV).

Paul travelled to Corinth to tell the people about Jesus. He also helped start a church so that all these new Christians could attend. But soon he found there was much fighting amongst them behaving like their old selves. Paul reminded them that they were now new in Christ and all the old ways of behaving was gone and they had a new way of behaving.

Find these words – look up, look down, look across and look diagonally, backwards and forwards.

Adventures	Corinth	Greece	New	People
Christ	Corinthians	Jesus	Old	Shipwreck
Christians	Creation	Malta	Passed	Time
Church	Fighting	Missionary	Paul	Travelled

Write below any additional words you find and compare with your friend.

N	A	S	S	A	Y	A	P	A	D	V	E	N	T	U	R	E	S	U	V
I	E	T	H	R	A	M	A	W	Q	A	J	J	C	D	S	N	E	W	Y
F	R	W	A	I	B	E	U	G	E	D	E	G	B	B	L	H	U	Y	Q
A	C	I	C	V	P	Y	L	I	O	S	S	V	O	R	X	B	A	I	T
C	W	O	O	R	J	W	Q	H	U	C	H	P	A	D	Y	S	C	Y	S
H	S	N	R	D	E	N	R	S	A	H	A	X	T	C	A	D	H	E	D
R	E	T	I	S	H	A	U	E	S	E	A	M	R	O	P	R	R	L	O
I	N	H	N	O	G	M	T	N	C	P	R	A	O	R	E	A	I	L	C
S	A	E	T	B	U	V	Y	I	E	K	K	L	B	I	N	W	S	O	P
T	S	O	H	E	O	C	B	E	O	T	N	T	O	N	Y	P	T	W	M
N	I	L	E	N	P	Y	G	M	R	N	S	A	G	T	I	U	I	O	V
Y	E	D	N	O	T	A	F	I	D	H	X	T	N	H	L	O	A	D	D
O	H	H	E	S	W	B	O	T	E	L	C	O	I	I	E	E	N	K	L
N	T	S	Y	T	Q	I	Y	H	S	D	O	M	T	A	S	C	S	E	O
E	S	R	H	S	E	D	E	S	S	A	P	E	H	N	S	E	T	L	Q
I	H	A	T	Y	X	O	R	N	G	N	U	N	G	S	X	E	Y	P	U
C	I	S	H	C	R	U	H	C	P	F	I	S	I	H	A	R	C	O	X
S	R	H	E	N	Z	A	E	Z	C	Q	V	D	F	Y	X	G	N	E	O
I	H	G	Y	R	A	N	O	I	S	S	I	M	X	Z	P	N	D	P	I
N	C	O	N	B	U	N	T	R	A	V	E	L	L	E	D	V	Q	A	E

10 Creative Art

Activities

MINI BEETLE KITE

You need

- 2 pieces of bamboo skewers or similar – 20cm and 16cm

- A4 white construction cardboard to draw beetle (20cm long/16cm wide)

- String approximately 70cm long

- Adhesive tape

- Colouring pencils or textas

- Black marker to outline beetle

- Scissors

Procedure

1. Draw or photocopy the template beetle as shown in picture on A4 paper using a pencil. Draw circles and lines where shown. When you are happy with the look of the beetle, go over it with a black marker.

2. Photocopy prototype or re-draw as many as you need for students.

3. Allow students to cut out their own beetle.

4. Decorate with colours of their choice. Write their name on the back.

5. Place 20cm stick on back of beetle horizontally. Using two 5cm pieces of tape, secure in place, top and bottom.

6. Place a 16cm stick on the back of beetle vertically. Using two 5cm pieces of tape, secure in place, left and right side.

7. Attach one end of the string to where the sticks cross over each other. Tie securely using a double knot.

8. Demonstrate to the students how to hold the string and fly their kite.

9. They can also take it home and hang on their walls.

MINI BEETLE KITE

PICTURE FRAME

You need

- Construction cardboard
  - Ruler
  - Pencil
  - Scissors
- Small decorations or pictures
  - Glue or glue stick
    - Glue brush
  - Picture of family
- Thin flat magnetic strip

Procedure

1. Draw or photocopy the template of two rectangular shapes sized 14cm horizontally and 18cm vertically.

2. On one of those shapes, come in from outside edge 3cm on each side marking the lines to create a smaller rectangle.

3. Cut out the inside of this rectangle to create your picture frame.

4. Using the inside of the frame, mark the two pieces of cardboard and have the students draw their family in between these lines or attach the photo in this spot. Direct students to write their names on the back.

5. On the cut out frame, brush the sides with glue and decorate.

6. When students are finished decorating, glue the back of the decorated frame and attach onto the cardboard with the family drawing.

7. Glue a thin flat magnetic strip on the back so students can put on their fridge.

PICTURE FRAME

FATHER'S DAY TIE

You need

- A4 construction cardboard
- Pencil
- Scissors
- Colouring pencils or textas
- Thin elastic string
- Adhesive tape or stapler

Procedure

1. Draw or photocopy the template of a man's tie using the full length of the A4 cardboard.

2. The top part of the tie needs to be a narrow tag approximately 5cm long.

3. Using scissors cut out the tie. Fold over narrow tag to create a loop and either tape it down or staple it down.

4. Thread through the loop a 50cm elastic string. Tie off to create a closed circle. Write names on the back of tie.

5. Direct students to decorate their tie with textas or pencils creating shapes and pictures.

YOU'RE
THE
BEST

FATHER'S DAY TIE

DOOR HANGER DECOUPAGE

You need

- Craft wood or thick cardboard cut to 25cm horizontally and 10cm vertically. Drill or cut a circle towards the top 6.5cm circumference and 2cm away from the top.

- Small-animated picture cut outs from wrapping paper or magazine.

- PVA glue

- Glue brush

- Scissors

- Pencil to write name on back

Procedure

1. Photocopy and cut out the template. Use as a guide for a timber cut out.

2. Invite student to write their name on the back of the door hanger.

3. Glue the front of the hanger and then place pictures on the board covering the whole area. Students may wish to cut out the picture defining a particular part of the picture.

4. Brush the glue on top of the picture to give it a hard surface when it dries.

DOOR HANGER DECOUPAGE

LEADLIGHT COLLAGE

You need

- A4 construction paper

- Transparency plastic or similar

- Adhesive Tape

- Cellophane in a variety of colours cut into small pieces

- PVA glue

- Glue brush

- Pencil

- Scissors

Procedure

1. Measure 4cm in from each outside edge and cut out to create a frame or photocopy the template.

2. Using tape, attach plastic to back of frame to secure in place.

3. Invite students to write their name on the back of the frame.

4.   Using glue, brush all over the clear plastic.

5.   Place different colours of cellophane all over the plastic creating a pattern of their choice until completely covered. Use scissors to cut cellophane in different shapes.

6.   Allow to dry. Place on a window where the sun comes through which will make the cellophane shine like a leadlight.

LEADLIGHT COLLAGE

PAPER DYING

You need

- Kitchen paper towels
- Food colouring in several bowls
- Eye droppers or similar
- Wooden peg
- String

Procedure

1. Fold paper about 8-10 times.

2. Dip one corner of the folded paper into one colour and lift out.

3. Dip another corner of the folded paper into another colour and lift out.

4. Repeat with all four corners of paper. Unfold and hang on a line with a peg to dry.

5. If you have access to an eyedropper, fill eyedropper with colour from one bowl and release over paper. Repeat this with other colours.

6. When dry, place a peg in the middle of the paper to create two wings and tie the string around the peg to hang from the ceiling.

PAPER DYING

BOOMERANG

You need

- Craft wood or thick construction paper
- A variety of legumes/beans
- PVA glue
- Glue brush
- Marker

Procedure

1. Photocopy the template and cut out the timber or construction paper in the shape of a boomerang. Ask the students to write their names on the back.

2. Section out a handful of legumes/beans for the students on each table.

3. Using a glue brush spread a generous amount of glue all over the boomerang.

4. Arrange the legumes/beans in a creative way. Allow to dry before taking home.

BOOMERANG

CHRISTMAS STAR

You need

- 2 colours of construction paper
- Glue
- Glitter
- Hand drawn picture of self or photo
- Hole puncher
- Ribbon 30cm long

Procedure

1. Photocopy the template and cut out two stars of two different colours for Christmas. Can be green and red, or silver and gold.
2. Cut inside of the star out leaving 2cm from the edge.
3. Glue the stars together allowing for points to go in between each other as shown in picture below.

4. Punch a hole on top of the star and thread the ribbon through to make a closed

circle. Tie off.

5. Brush the glue on the star and sprinkle with glitter. Allow to dry before taking

home.

CHRISTMAS STAR

UNIVERSE MOBILE

You need

- A variety of coloured construction paper

- Small paper plate

- Hole puncher

- Ribbon

- Glitter

- Colouring pencils or textas

Procedure

1. Cut out the paper plate like a sun with rays as in picture.

2. Photocopy the template and cut out a moon, sun and planets, as many as you like.

3. Punch a hole in the top of the sun and thread a 20cm ribbon through. Tie off into a loop.

4. Place 4 holes in the bottom of the sun and attach another four 20cm ribbons through. Tie off. Punch a hole through the moon, sun, planets and tie off with hanging ribbons.

5. Place a small amount of glue on the cut outs and sprinkle with glitter, or decorate with pencils or both. Allow to dry before hanging.

UNIVERSE MOBILE

A WHALE OF A FISH

You need

- A4 cardboard

- A4 white paper

- Colouring pencils or textas

- Scissors

- Glue stick

- Crepe paper

- Beach sand

Procedure

1. Photocopy the template and cut out the pattern for the fish, setting aside the water spout, the tail and the body using the A4 white paper.

2. Colour in whale using pencils or textas.

3. Glue the body on the A4 cardboard, then glue spout and tail at an angle.

4. Ask the students to write their name on the top of the cardboard.

5. Using crepe paper or coloured paper, create 10cm twists representing seaweed coming up from the bottom, using glue to secure.

6. Place some glue along the bottom of the paper and sprinkle some beach sand to create a coastal scene.

A WHALE OF A FISH

Templates

For

Creative Art

Activities

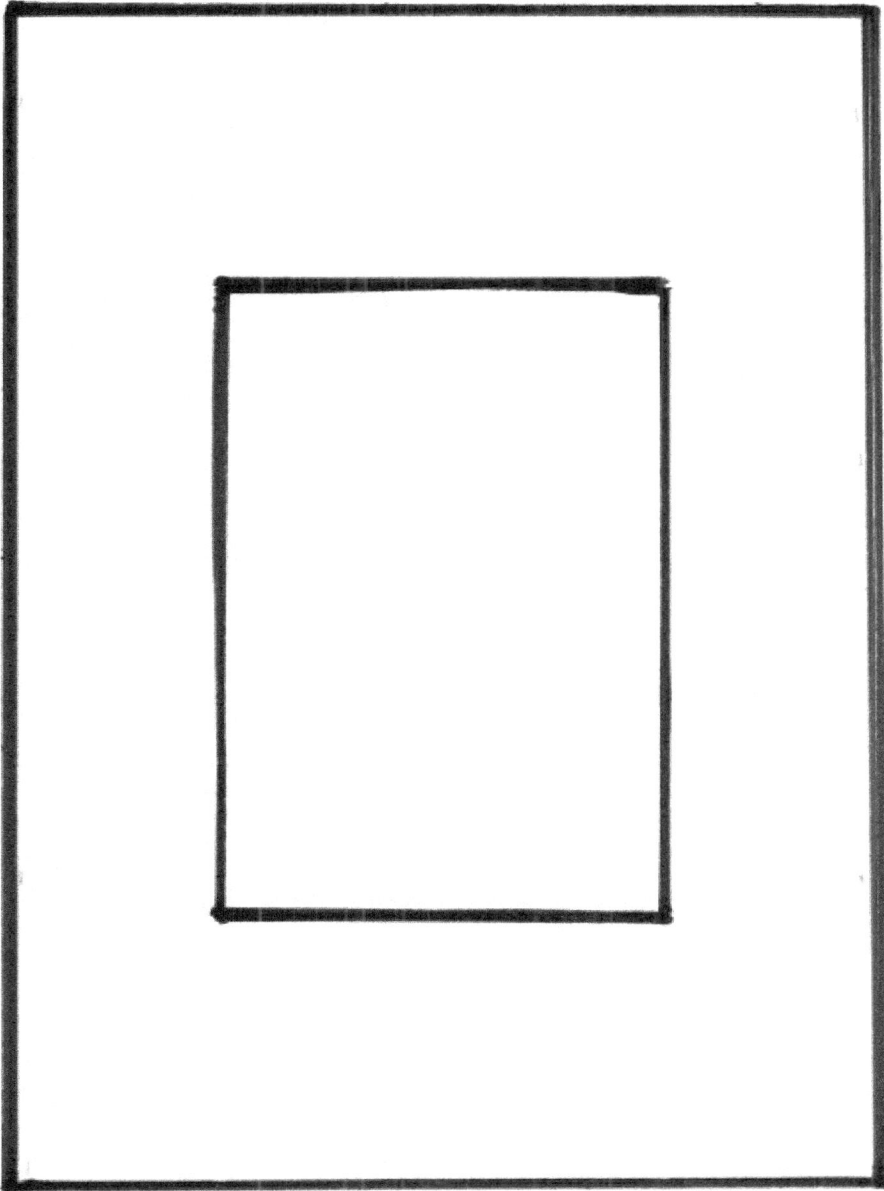

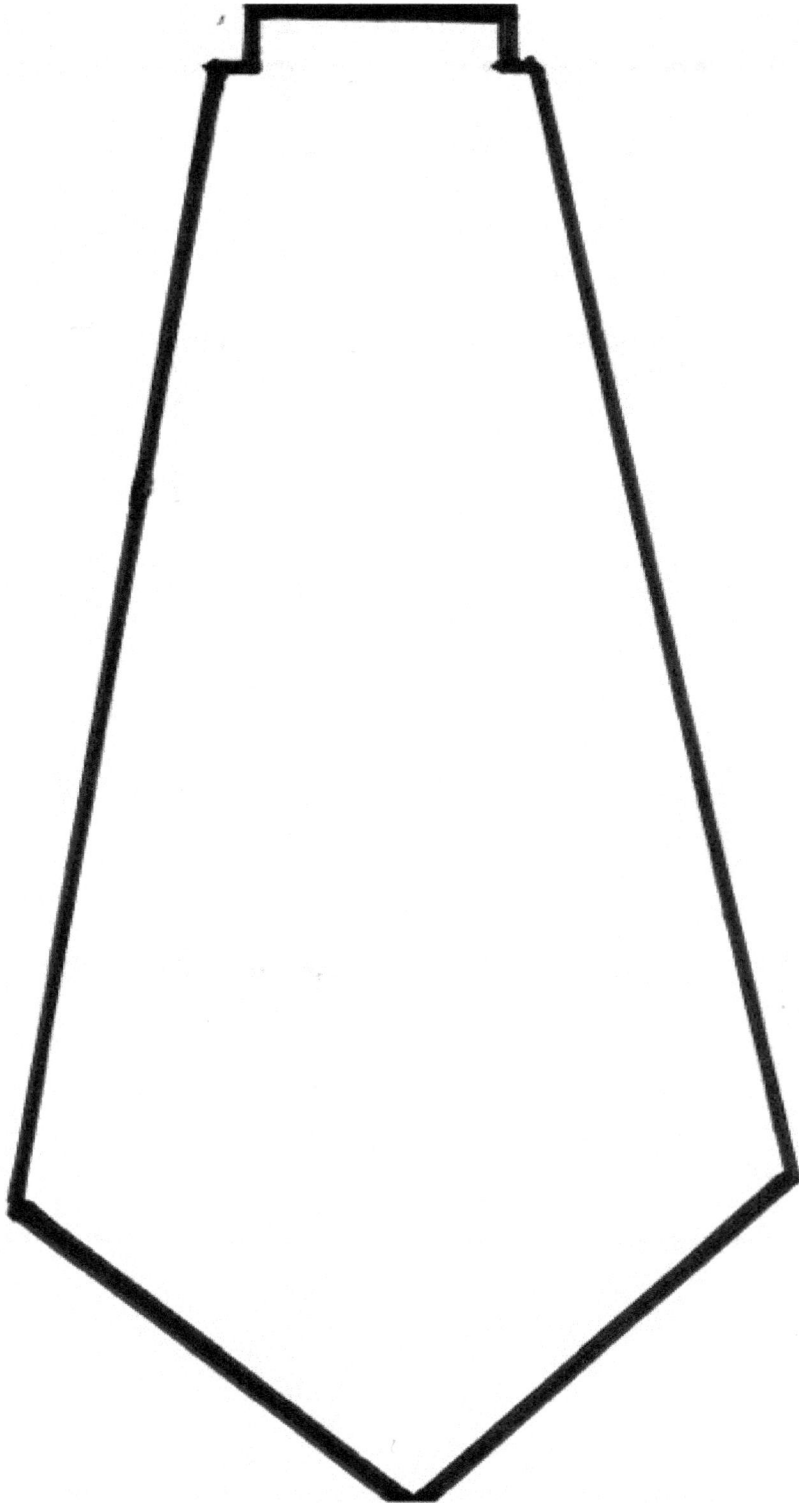

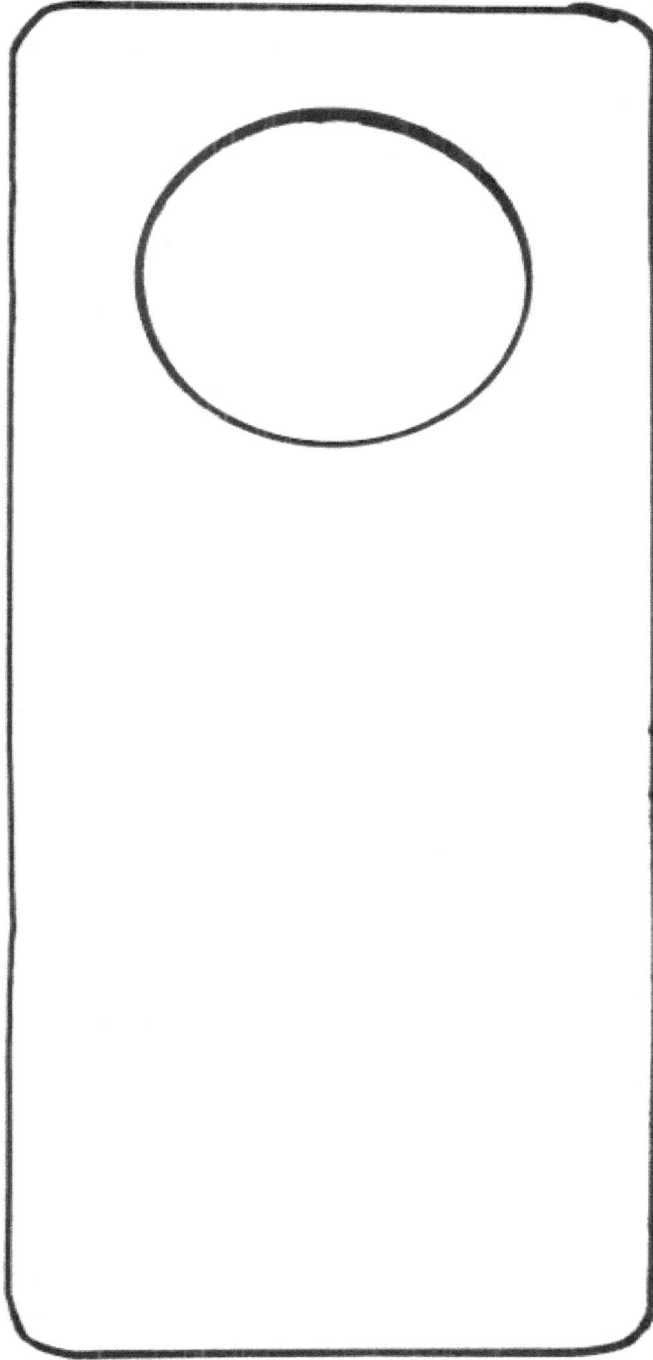

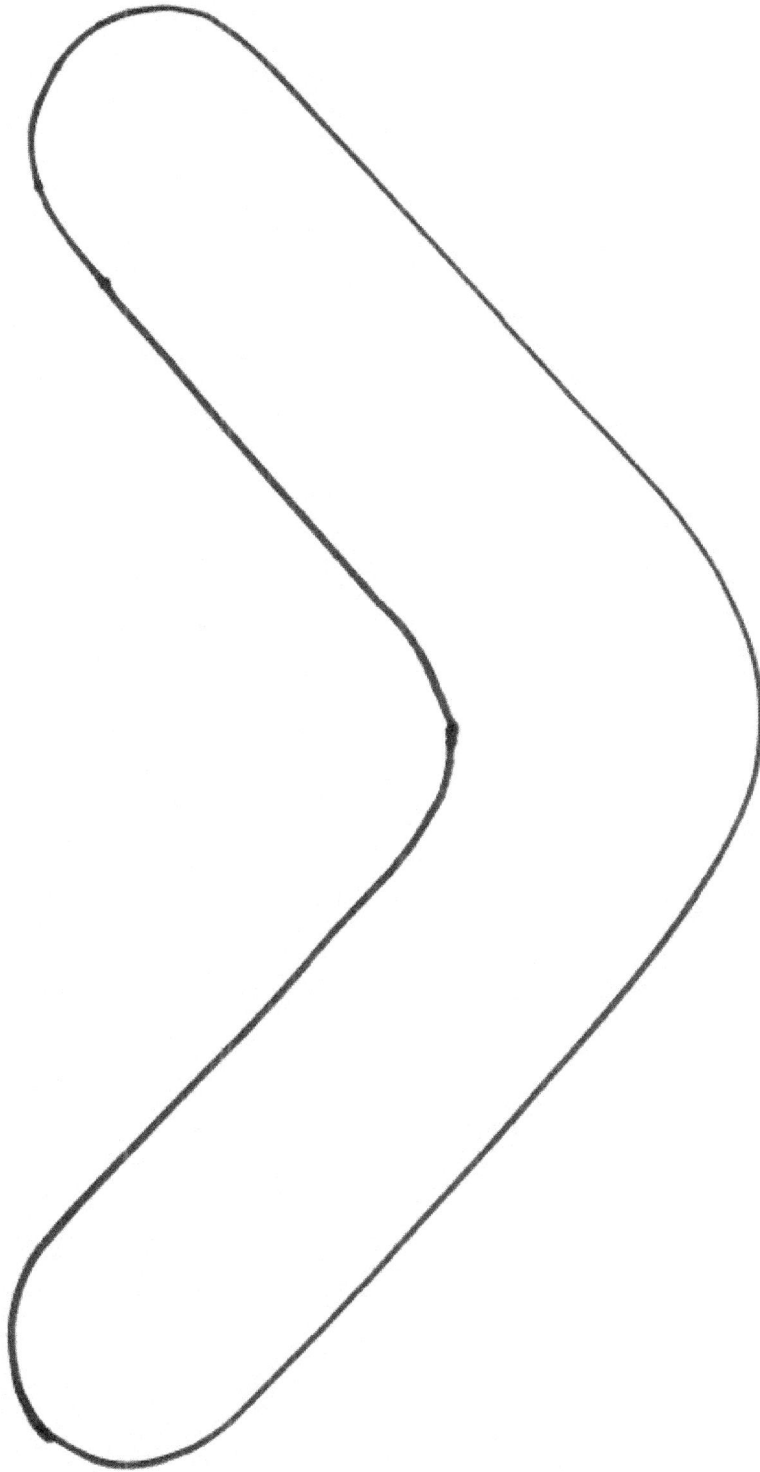

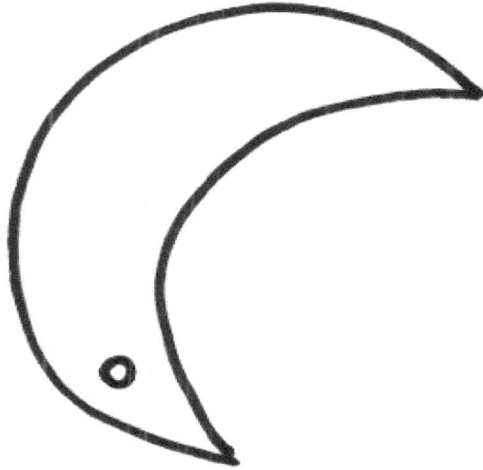

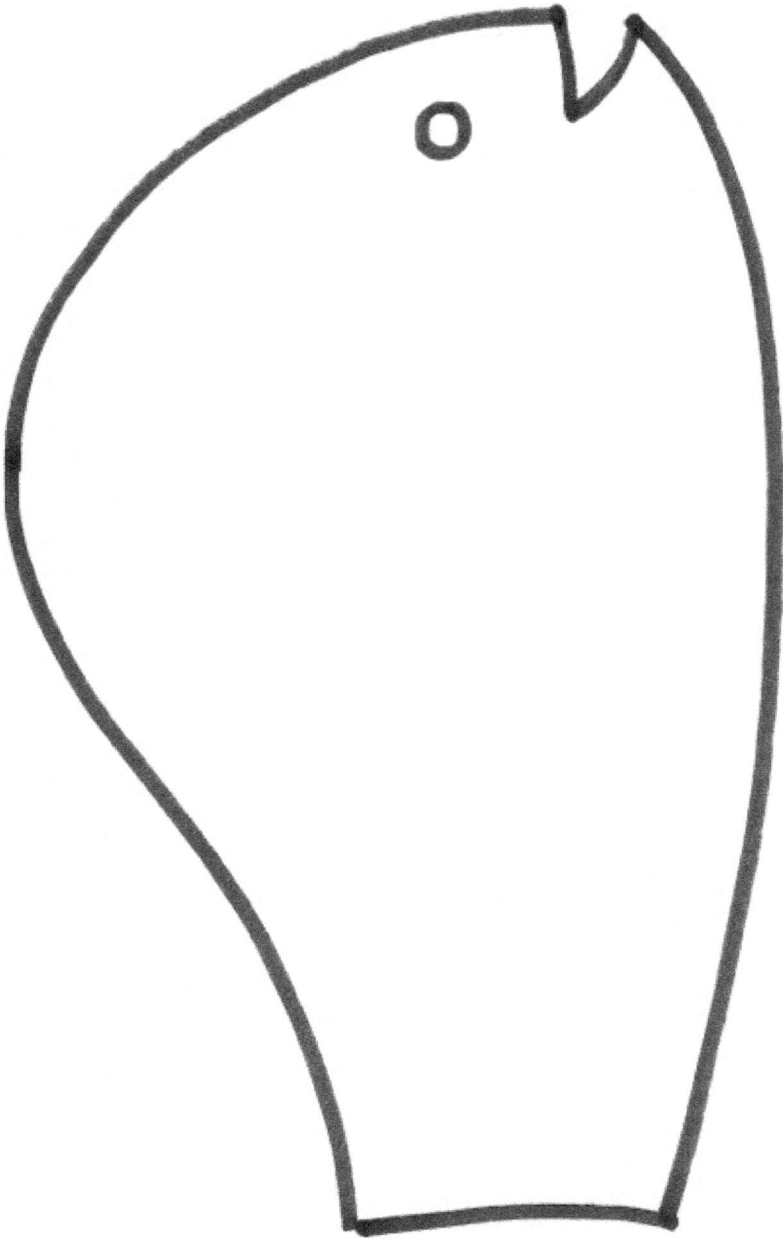

5 Explosive Science

Experiments

THE EXPLOSIVE VOLCANO

You will need

- Large dish or tray
- Vinegar
- Funnel
- Small bottle
- Bicarbonate of soda
- A bucket of sand & gravel
- Red food colouring

Procedure

1. Place the small bottle in the middle of the tray.

2. Fill the tray with sand and gravel creating a mountain around the bottle but not covering the opening of the bottle.

3. Add red food colouring into the vinegar.

4. Insert funnel into the bottle and half fill with bicarbonate soda.

5. Pour some red vinegar into the bottle and stand back and watch the explosive show!

BALLOON BLAST

You will need

- Balloons
- Adhesive tape
- Straws
- String

Procedure

1. Cut a length of string about 8-10 metres long.

2. Invite two students to come forward and hold each end of the string.

3. Thread a straw on one end of the string.

4. Blow up the balloon and twist the neck but do not tie it up or let go.

5. Tape the balloon to the straw with the opening facing the opposite way you want it to go.

6. Count backwards starting from 10 and then release the balloon to blast its way to the other end of the string.

7. The balloon will travel along the string until all the air has been released from the balloon.

COLOUR EXPLOSIONS

You will need

- Large dish or tray
- Milk
- A variety of food colouring
- Eye-dropper or similar
- Detergent
- Blotting paper or similar

Procedure

1. Pour milk to fill the bottom of the dish or tray.
2. Add a few drops of different food colouring.
3. Add a drop of detergent and watch for the explosion of colours.
4. Gently press one side of the blotting paper on the surface of the water and capture all the colours on the paper.
5. Lay paper on non-painted side and allow to dry and use for another activity of your choice.

THE SPINNING TORNADO

You will need

- 2 empty soft drink bottles
- Electrical or packing tape
- Food colouring
- Glitter
- Water

Procedure

1. Fill one bottle with water, a drop of food colouring and some glitter.

2. Place the other bottle on top, openings facing each other.

3. Wrap the tape around necks of both bottles to seal together and make one object.

4. Spin bottle around and watch for the tornado to form.

EXPLODING BALLOONS

You will need

- 1 empty soft drink bottle
- Bicarbonate of soda
- Vinegar
- Deflated balloons
- Funnel
- Tray

Procedure

1. Pour vinegar into the soft drink bottle until it is one-third full.
2. Place the funnel into the deflated balloon and fill it with the bicarbonate of soda.
3. Stretch the opening of the balloon over the neck of the bottle and firmly attach.
4. Lift the filled balloon so that the bicarbonate of soda falls into the bottle.
5. The vinegar will begin to react with the bicarbonate of soda and watch the balloon start to inflate.

www.ingramcontent.com/pod-product-compliance
Lightning Source LLC
Chambersburg PA
CBHW081426090426
42740CB00017B/3198

9780992437114